BLAZERS

Wild
Outdoors

Deer Hunting

by Thomas K. Adamson

Reading Consultant: Barbara J. Fox
Reading Specialist
North Carolina State University

Content Consultant: Greg Slone
Next Generation Hunting
Bowling Green, Kentucky

CAPSTONE PRESS
a capstone imprint

Blazers is published by Capstone Press,
151 Good Counsel Drive, P.O. Box 669, Mankato, Minnesota 56002.
www.capstonepub.com

 Books published by Capstone Press are manufactured with paper
containing at least 10 percent post-consumer waste.

Library of Congress Cataloging-in-Publication Data
Adamson, Thomas K., 1970-
  Deer hunting / by Thomas K. Adamson.
    p. cm.—(Blazers. Wild outdoors)
  Includes bibliographical references and index.
  ISBN 978-1-4296-4807-3 (library binding)
  1. Deer hunting—Juvenile literature. I. Title. II. Series.

SK301.A274 2011
799.2'7652—dc22   2009053412

Editorial Credits
Christine Peterson, editor; Veronica Correia, designer; Sarah Schuette, photo stylist;
    Marcy Morin, scheduler; Laura Manthe, production specialist

Photo Credits
Capstone Studio/Karon Dubke, all photos except:
fotolia: Charles Kaye, 29; Shutterstock: Mike Rogal, 23, Timothy R. Nichols, 7

Artistic Effects
Capstone Press/Karon Dubke (woods); Shutterstock: rvika (wood), rvrspb (fence), VikaSuh (sign)

Printed in the United States of America in Stevens Point, Wisconsin.
092010
005957R

Table of Contents

Chapter 1
Waiting for the Right Shot 4

Chapter 2
Equipment 8

Chapter 3
Skills and Techniques 18

Chapter 4
Safety 24

Chapter 5
An Outdoor Adventure! 28

Equipment Diagram 16

Glossary. 30

Read More 31

Internet Sites 31

Index 32

Waiting for the Right Shot

You wait silently in your hunting stand. A huge deer comes into view. But you don't shoot. You wait patiently for the perfect shot.

Wild Fact:

North American deer include white-tailed deer, mule deer, elk, moose, and caribou.

The deer comes closer to your stand. It sniffs the air. Can it smell you? Suddenly, it darts off. You'll have to wait for another shot.

Wild Fact:

White-tailed deer can run 40 miles (64 kilometers) per hour.

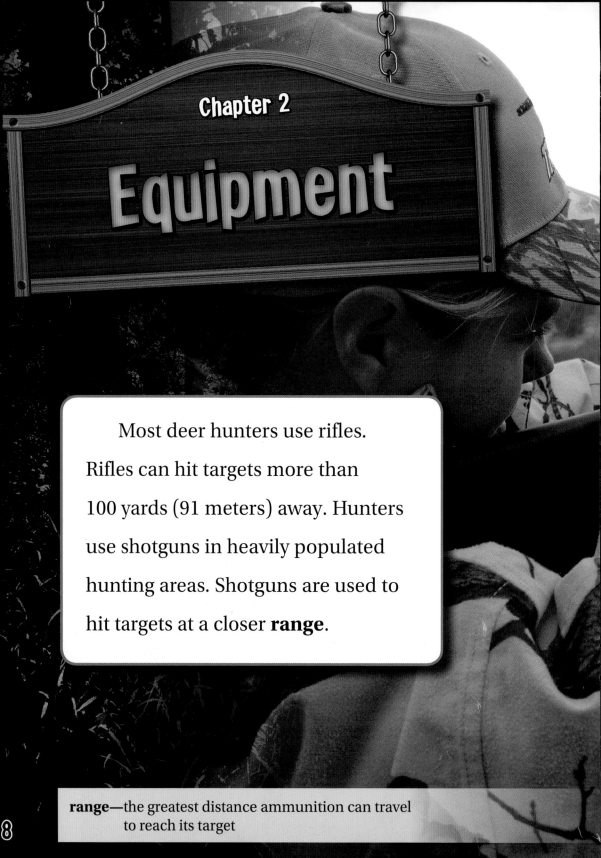

Chapter 2

Equipment

Most deer hunters use rifles. Rifles can hit targets more than 100 yards (91 meters) away. Hunters use shotguns in heavily populated hunting areas. Shotguns are used to hit targets at a closer **range**.

range—the greatest distance ammunition can travel to reach its target

Wild Fact:

The best spot to hit a deer is behind its shoulder near the rib cage.

Hunters attach scopes to their guns. Deer hunters use **scopes** to get a closer look at their targets. Scopes also help hunters make **accurate** shots at deer.

scope

scope—a piece of equipment that makes faraway objects appear closer
accurate—able to hit the target at which a hunter aims

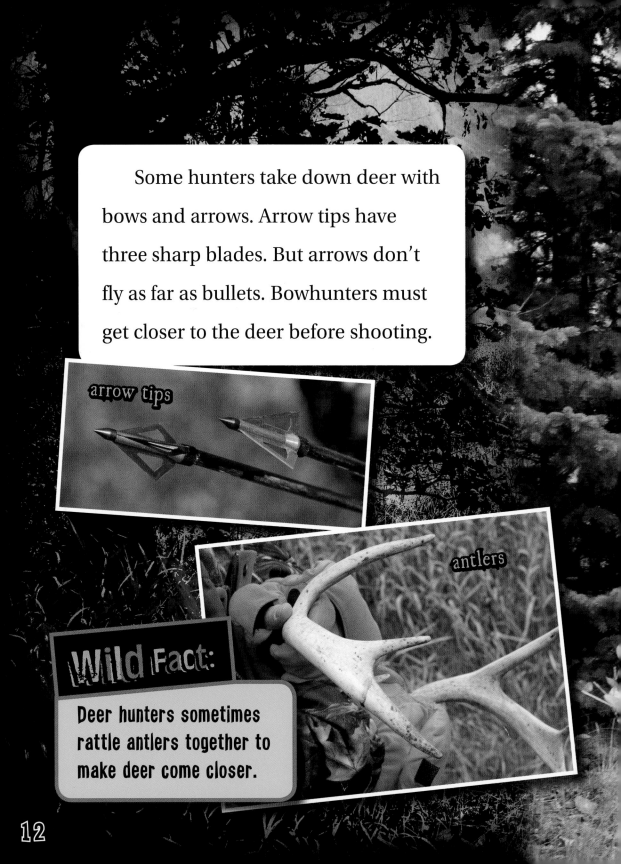

Some hunters take down deer with bows and arrows. Arrow tips have three sharp blades. But arrows don't fly as far as bullets. Bowhunters must get closer to the deer before shooting.

arrow tips

antlers

Wild Fact:

Deer hunters sometimes rattle antlers together to make deer come closer.

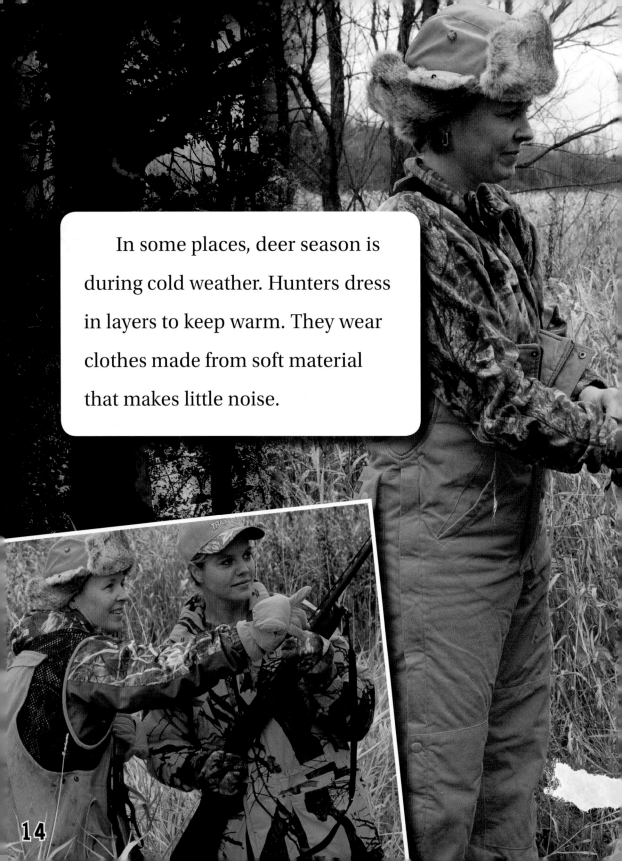

In some places, deer season is during cold weather. Hunters dress in layers to keep warm. They wear clothes made from soft material that makes little noise.

Deer Hunting Equipment

blaze orange clothing

gloves

hunting knives

gun case

hunting antlers

compound
bow

hat

scent
prevent

scope

call

shells

rifle

hunting license

binoculars

rifle cartridges

arrows

camouflage
clothing

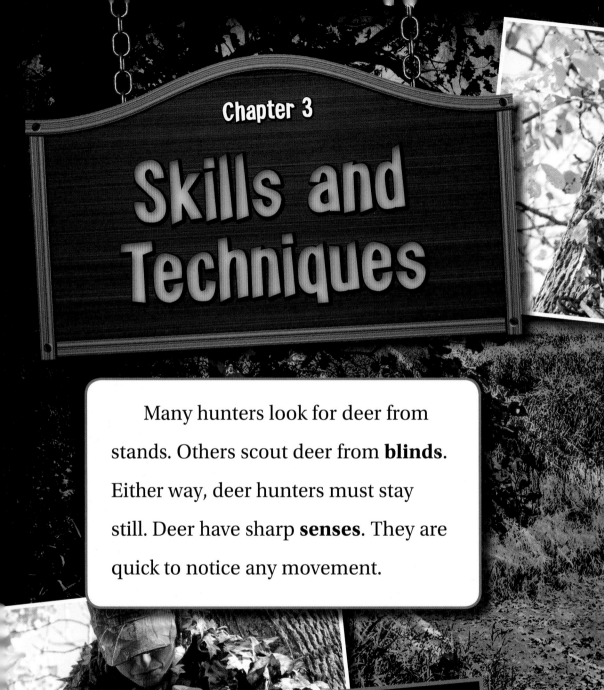

Chapter 3

Skills and Techniques

Many hunters look for deer from stands. Others scout deer from **blinds**. Either way, deer hunters must stay still. Deer have sharp **senses**. They are quick to notice any movement.

harness

Wild Fact:

In stands, hunters should wear harnesses to prevent falls.

stand

blind—a hidden place from which deer hunters can shoot deer

sense—a way of knowing about your surroundings

19

Wild Fact:

Animals can smell your breath.
Some hunters chew odorless gum.

Hunters use the wind to help them hide from their prey. Hunters walk into the wind. The wind carries their odor away from deer.

Some hunters cover themselves in doe urine and **scents**. They also place scents near their treestand or blind. These smells attract deer and hide a hunter's odor.

scent—an odor

Wild Fact:

Deer are 4,000 times more sensitive to odors than people are.

Chapter 4

Safety

Hunters stay safe when using guns. They keep the gun **safety** on until they are ready to shoot. Hunters never point their gun at another person. They make sure their target is a deer before shooting.

gun safety

safety—a device that prevents a gun from firing

Wild Fact:

Hunters don't load their guns until they are ready to hunt. They unload their guns when they are done hunting.

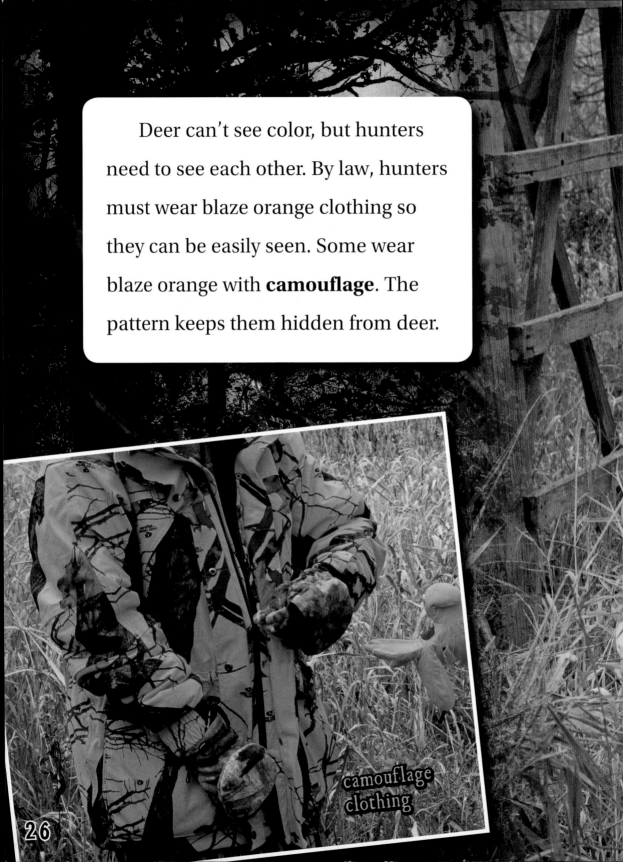

Deer can't see color, but hunters need to see each other. By law, hunters must wear blaze orange clothing so they can be easily seen. Some wear blaze orange with **camouflage**. The pattern keeps them hidden from deer.

camouflage clothing

camouflage—coloring that helps hunters blend in with their surroundings

Chapter 5

An Outdoor Adventure!

Deer hunting takes patience, skill, and a little luck. Hunters spend hours in the woods in hopes of bringing home a huge buck. Are you ready to try this outdoor adventure?

Wild Fact:

Deer hunters must buy a license in order to hunt legally.

Glossary

accurate (AK-yuh-ruht)—able to hit the target at which a hunter aimed

blind (BLYND)—a hidden place from which hunters can shoot prey

camouflage (KA-muh-flahzh)—coloring that makes hunters blend in with their surroundings

range (RAYNJ)—the greatest distance ammunition can travel to reach its target

safety (SAYF-tee)—a device that prevents a gun from firing

scent (SENT)—the odor or smell of something

scope (SKOHP)—a piece of equipment that makes faraway objects appear closer

sense (SENSS)—a way of knowing about your surroundings; hearing, smelling, touching, tasting, and sight are the five senses

stand (STAND)—a raised platform hunters use to get a better view of their hunting area; some hunting stands are built in trees

Read More

Frahm, Randy. *Deer Hunting.* Great Outdoors. Mankato, Minn.: Capstone Press, 2008.

Macken, JoAnn Early. *Deer.* Animals that Live in the Forest. Pleasantville, N.Y.: Gareth Stevens Publishing, 2010.

Mara, Wil. *Deer.* Animals Animals. New York: Marshall Cavendish Benchmark, 2008.

Wilson, Jef. *Hunting for Fun!* For Fun! Minneapolis: Compass Point Books, 2006.

Internet Sites

FactHound offers a safe, fun way to find Internet sites related to this book. All of the sites on FactHound have been researched by our staff.

Here's all you do:

Visit *www.facthound.com*

Type in this code: **9781429648073**

Index

antlers, 12
arrows, 12

blinds, 18, 22
bows, 12

clothing, 14, 26
    blaze orange, 26
    camouflage, 26

deer, 4, 6, 7, 9, 11, 12, 18, 21, 22,
        24, 28
    kinds of, 4, 28

gun safety, 24

harnesses, 18
hunting safety, 24, 25, 26

laws, 26
licenses, 28

rifles, 8

scents, 21, 22, 23
scopes, 11
senses, 18
shotguns, 8
stands, 4, 6, 18, 22

wind, 21